I0154919

Pug Dogs as Pets

Everything You Need to Know about
Pug Dogs

Pug Dogs Characteristics, Health, Diet, Breeding,
Types, Buying, Showing, Care and a whole lot more!

By Lolly Brown

Copyrights and Trademarks

All rights reserved. No part of this book may be reproduced or transformed in any form or by any means, graphic, electronic, or mechanical, including photocopying, recording, taping, or by any information storage retrieval system, without the written permission of the author.

This publication is Copyright ©2017 NRB Publishing, an imprint of Pack & Post Plus, LLC. Nevada. All products, graphics, publications, software and services mentioned and recommended in this publication are protected by trademarks. In such instance, all trademarks & copyright belong to the respective owners. For information consult www.NRBpublishing.com

Disclaimer and Legal Notice

This product is not legal, medical, or accounting advice and should not be interpreted in that manner. You need to do your own due-diligence to determine if the content of this product is right for you. While every attempt has been made to verify the information shared in this publication, neither the author, neither publisher, nor the affiliates assume any responsibility for errors, omissions or contrary interpretation of the subject matter herein. Any perceived slights to any specific person(s) or organization(s) are purely unintentional.

We have no control over the nature, content and availability of the web sites listed in this book. The inclusion of any web site links does not necessarily imply a recommendation or endorse the views expressed within them. We take no responsibility for, and will not be liable for, the websites being temporarily unavailable or being removed from the internet.

The accuracy and completeness of information provided herein and opinions stated herein are not guaranteed or warranted to produce any particular results, and the advice and strategies, contained herein may not be suitable for every individual. Neither the author nor the publisher shall be liable for any loss incurred as a consequence of the use and application, directly or indirectly, of any information presented in this work. This publication is designed to provide information in regard to the subject matter covered.

Neither the author nor the publisher assume any responsibility for any errors or omissions, nor do they represent or warrant that the ideas, information, actions, plans, suggestions contained in this book is in all cases accurate. It is the reader's responsibility to find advice before putting anything written in this book into practice. The information in this book is not intended to serve as legal, medical, or accounting advice.

Foreword

The cubby, swirly-tailed, bug-eyed Pug has been around for a relatively long time and has consistently been listed as one of America's favorite choice for pets. Perhaps the continued popularity this smart little guy enjoys is owed to its easygoing demeanor, its good sense of humor, or maybe it's because of his keen sensitivity toward his human emotions which make the Pug a highly sought after breed of companion dog.

The Pug, in all its tiny glory, has indeed been a canine who was, and is continued to be, chosen by many nobilities, royalties, notable people of influence as well as regular, everyday families and individuals who share a deep love and admiration for the breed.

In this book you'll learn a Pug's characteristics, behaviors, health issues, nutrition tips, breeding, maintenance, and how you can be the greatest Pug owner ever.

Table of Contents

Introduction

The information herein is aimed to give insight and important information you need whether you are still in the deciding stage or eagerly expecting the arrival of the new addition to your home. Other than readily accessible information collected and collated by more recent observers of the Pug very little is known about how this wrinkly, playful canine came about into existence. Its parents were never identified - or if they were, never documented.

Despite the gap in information, the Pug after gaining favour and fame amongst Chinese royalty went on to be one of the three breeds of snubbed-nosed canines known to have been bred by the people of China as companions or employed as a guard dog. The two other canines developed would be the Pekinese and the Lion dog. Back then, the Pug of ancient China was called the Lo-sze.

There are those who think that the popular "Foo Dogs" of China are depictions of the Pugs. Others would argue that these "dogs" are in fact lions. Evidence had been discovered of the existence of Pug-like dogs in ancient Japan and Tibet. Tibetan Buddhist monks kept them as pets in monasteries when the breed later spread out and found themselves in other parts of Asia. These are strong indicators of the Pu, further making its way out of China.

It has, however, definitely been established that these larger-than-life canines are direct descendants of the lovable lap dogs imported to European shores from the vast, historical lands of China in the 16th century. No matter the vagueness of its advent into human homes as companions, one constant is ever present - the Pug has been around for a very long time and has been recorded to have played crucial roles in histories of the ancients. The playful Pug, in ancient Chinese times, was bred to be loyal companions and was meant to accompany the ruling families of China. These adorable Pugs were taken in as pets by powerful Chinese Emperors. This breed of canine was greatly valued and was guardedly taken care of in luxury under the watchful eye of soldiers detailed to ensure the safety of these favored dogs.

They have been constantly sought after by small and big families, whether with or without children. It has been a kind and mindful companion for elderly folk who neither have the energy nor the patience to deal with the antics of a hyper-active canine.

It is an amusing, tiny little creature packed to the hilt and brimming over with love and amusing tactics that will capture the heart and attention of its guardian.

Glossary of Dog Terms

AKC – American Kennel Club, the largest purebred dog registry in the United States

Almond Eye – Referring to an elongated eye shape rather than a rounded shape

Apple Head – A round-shaped skull

Balance – A show term referring to all of the parts of the dog, both moving and standing, which produce a harmonious image

Beard – Long, thick hair on the dog's underjaw

Best in Show – An award given to the only undefeated dog left standing at the end of judging

Bitch – A female dog

Bite – The position of the upper and lower teeth when the dog's jaws are closed; positions include level, undershot, scissors, or overshot

Blaze – A white stripe running down the center of the face between the eyes

Board – To house, feed, and care for a dog for a fee

Breed – A domestic race of dogs having a common gene pool and characterized appearance/function

Breed Standard – A published document describing the look, movement, and behavior of the perfect specimen of a particular breed

Buff – An off-white to gold coloring

Clip – A method of trimming the coat in some breeds

Coat – The hair covering of a dog; some breeds have two coats, and outer coat and undercoat; also known as a double coat. Examples of breeds with double coats include German Shepherd, Siberian Husky, Akita, etc.

Condition – The health of the dog as shown by its skin, coat, behavior, and general appearance

Crate – A container used to house and transport dogs; also called a cage or kennel

Crossbreed (Hybrid) – A dog having a sire and dam of two different breeds; cannot be registered with the AKC

Dam (bitch) – The female parent of a dog;

Dock – To shorten the tail of a dog by surgically removing the end part of the tail.

Double Coat – Having an outer weather-resistant coat and a soft, waterproof coat for warmth; see above.

Drop Ear – An ear in which the tip of the ear folds over and hangs down; not prick or erect

Entropion – A genetic disorder resulting in the upper or lower eyelid turning in

Fancier – A person who is especially interested in a particular breed or dog sport

Fawn – A red-yellow hue of brown

Feathering – A long fringe of hair on the ears, tail, legs, or body of a dog

Groom – To brush, trim, comb or otherwise make a dog's coat neat in appearance

Heel – To command a dog to stay close by its owner's side

Hip Dysplasia – A condition characterized by the abnormal formation of the hip joint

Inbreeding – The breeding of two closely related dogs of one breed

Kennel – A building or enclosure where dogs are kept

Litter – A group of puppies born at one time

Markings – A contrasting color or pattern on a dog's coat

Mask – Dark shading on the dog's foreface

Mate – To breed a dog and a bitch

Neuter – To castrate a male dog or spay a female dog

Pads – The tough, shock-absorbent skin on the bottom of a dog's foot

Parti-Color – A coloration of a dog's coat consisting of two or more definite, well-broken colors; one of the colors must be white

Pedigree – The written record of a dog's genealogy going back three generations or more

Pied – A coloration on a dog consisting of patches of white and another color

Prick Ear – Ear that is carried erect, usually pointed at the tip of the ear

Puppy – A dog under 12 months of age

Purebred – A dog whose sire and dam belong to the same breed and who are of unmixed descent

Saddle – Colored markings in the shape of a saddle over the back; colors may vary

Shedding – The natural process whereby old hair falls off the dog's body as it is replaced by new hair growth.

Sire – The male parent of a dog

Smooth Coat – Short hair that is close-lying

Spay – The surgery to remove a female dog's ovaries, rendering her incapable of breeding

Trim – To groom a dog's coat by plucking or clipping

Undercoat – The soft, short coat typically concealed by a longer outer coat

Wean – The process through which puppies transition from subsisting on their mother's milk to eating solid food

Whelping – The act of birthing a litter of puppies

Chapter One: Pugs in Focus

Pugs are well known as amiably sociable and tender companion dogs and they have been the choice pet for many titled royalty, aristocratic personages and common folk of yore and today. Although depicted in 18th century prints to be lean and long, today's modern day partiality has favored and leaned more toward the appearance of the breed; demanding for a compact form, a cubby, square body, a deep chest with well-formed muscles of balanced proportion.

The smooth glossy coats of these well-loved canines come in varying shades of apricot fawn, silver fawn, fawn or black. The coat markings are visibly defined with a hint of a black line extending from the occiput to the canine's tail. The unique tail of the Pug typically tightly curls over its hip.

There are two evident shapes for the Pug's ears; button and rose. The standard button-shaped ears are folded with the front edge of the ears resting against the sides of its head whilst the rose-shaped ears are notably smaller. Breeding preference, stated on the Pug Dog Club of America archives, favors the button-style ears over the rosebud-shaped ears of the Pug.

The legs of the Pug are noted to be sturdy, functionally straight, are of moderate length and well set under its carriage. The shoulder of the Pug is laid back moderately. The ankles are strong with small feet and their toes are split-up well. The nails are naturally black. The distinctly significant look of the Pug is due to the further protrusion of their lower teeth than their upper teeth - which results in the dog's unmistakable look with its slightly pronounced under bite.

The Pug is one of the most remarkably charming canine personalities you will ever come across. The Latin phrase 'multum in parvo' or "a lot of dog in a small space" alludes to its overall characteristics notwithstanding its small size. Pugs are rarely aggressive but they are strong-willed. They are suitable for families who have older children as well as individuals who may not be physically active enough to be paired with a larger, much more active canine. The greater majority of this breed is quite fond of children and is strong enough to withstand proper play with young ones.

These dogs can be silent and meek, depending on their guardians moods, but they can also be teasing and vivacious little critters. Pugs are known to be intuitive and sensitive to the moods and emotions their caregivers experience and will eagerly try to please their caregivers at such times.

Pugs are widely known to be a tad lazy and will spend a lot of time napping and lounging when not socializing or in active play. They have been dubbed as "shadows" because they like to get into the bustle of everyday activities and enjoy being in the thick of family interactions. They are popular affection-seekers and attention-getters from their guardians.

Facts about Pugs

The remarkably charming Pug Dog is a breed of canine that is uniquely different in temperament and physique. Sporting a wrinkly, snub-muzzled face, a strong chubby physique set on sturdy legs with a noticeably curled tail, has been called quite a bit of names since its introduction to society many centuries ago.

This canine breed has a glossy coat which comes in a variety of colors, notably in black or fawn and has a square and compact body with strong well-developed muscles. Pugs are bred as companions and this is the job they love and do best. Do not expect the generally languid Pug to fetch or retrieve anything. The Pug is happiest to amuse you with its own brand of puppy antics and tomfoolery.

Your lap - and love - is what the Pug craves the most just as much as it will crave your attention. It will express unhappiness if the devotion it gives is not returned and reciprocated by its caregiver. It has a tendency to live a sedentary life, happy to sit on your chest or lap as you enjoy a good book or your favorite show. This is not to say that the Pug is a boring dog. On the contrary, it is a comically playful canine that enjoys gaiety and delights its caregiver with silly fandango that will surely elicit a chuckle or two.

Brought in from China to Europe in the 16th century, Pugs were made popular in Western Europe by the House of Stuart in Scotland and the House of Orange of the Netherlands. Queen Victoria, in the 19th century developed a strong attraction to Pugs and she passed this passion to other members of the Royal Family who carried on caring for a series of Pugs throughout their reign. Not only are Pugs sought after today by many canine lovers, they have also been a constant choice for Imperial courts, royalties and noble-people alike as evidenced in portraits, frescoes, paintings and carvings, they are still widely popular today for their friendly traits that have endeared them to many canine aficionados.

A Pug, lovingly called Pompey was crucial in saving the life of the Prince of Orange when it gave warning by alerting the Prince to the presence of approaching assassins. The beloved dog later became the official canine of the House of Orange and enjoyed the perks of a hero.

It was a Pug who accompanied the travels of William III and Mary II in 1688, who both left the Netherlands to claim and accept the throne of England. It was possible that the Pug, during this time, may have been bred with the old sort of King Charles Spaniel which gave the modern King Charles spaniel its Pug-like characteristics.

This canine breed gained great popularity in many other European countries and was highly sought after by noble men and women of that era as pet companions. They were subjects of a few art works done by the painter Francisco Goya in Spain. The favored Pugs were transported via private carriages in Italy as they rode upfront, donning pantaloons and jackets, all of which matched those of the attending coachman. They were employed by the military of that time to track people and animals and were commonly utilized as guard dogs.

A devoted Pug lover and caregiver of a series of Pug dogs, painter William Hogarth, in 1745 included his Pug named Trump in a self-portrait. This timeless rendition of the duo is now displayed in London's Tate Gallery. The Pug was also very present and highly visible in many Italian locales and this is proven true by a discovered journal entry of a Mrs. Piozzi who scribed a personal observation. She discloses in her writings that the amiable canine may have left London to grace Padua, Italy due to the frequent sighting and visibility of the Pug canine in the streets of the Italian city.

Its fame eventually spread to nearby France in the 18th century when the first wife of Napoleon I, and first Empress of the French, Joséphine de Beauharnais, who before marrying Napoleon was imprisoned but was allowed one visitor. During the period of her imprisonment she was regularly visited by her Pug dog. It was during these visits when she secretly hid notes and used the canine to transport notes of communication to her family and vice versa. Under the patronage of Queen Victoria of England, the breed flourished even more in the 19th century. She bred many of these Pugs herself which included the Pugs she named Venus, Fatima, Minka, Olga and Pedro. Her close and active participation with the canines in general aided in the establishment of the Kennel Club, which was founded in 1873. During his period of time, countless aficionados reciprocated to the canine breeds' bantam size and its image of anti-functionalist. Preferring to keep the dogs as lap companions rather than employing them as trackers or guard dogs as other caregivers before them did.

Pugs, in engravings and paintings of the 18th and 19th centuries, usually appeared with longer limbs and noses than what we are used to seeing today. Sometimes they even appeared to have cropped ears.

It is supposed that the modern Pugs looks may have seen a change after 1860 when a new series of Pugs were directly imported from China. These new wave of Pugs from China sported shorter fore and hind quarters and they had the more modern Pug nose we see today.

Lady Brassey, a British aristocrat, is considered as the personality who made fashionable some of the black coloured Pugs she had brought back from China in 1886. Pug dogs landed on United States shores during the 19th century and soon made their way into loving homes and eventually, countless rings of American dog shows.

It was specifically after the United States Civil War when Pugs made their debut in American shores. The breed was later recognized by the American Kennel Club in 1885. The onset of the American introduction of Pugs saw great favour for the breed amongst dog-lovers. However, the turn of the century saw a decline in interest toward the breed. Due to the persistence of some dedicated breeders who continued to breed them, the Pug once again regained footing on the canine popularity list and was reintroduced to society and dog aficionados all over. It was in 1931 when the Pug Dog Club of America (PDCA) was founded and given recognition by the American Kennel Club.

The Pug, Dhandys Favourite Woodchuck, in 1981 won the Westminster Kennel Dog Show in the US - it is the only Pug to win there since the inception of the show in 1877. A Pug, called Double D Cinoblu's Masterpiece, was named The Best in Show or The World Champion at the 2004 World Dog Show, which was held in the city of Rio de Janeiro in Brazil.

Summary of Pugs in Facts

- Scientific Name: Canis lupus familiaris
- Breed Size: small-sized
- Height: 10 inches to 1 foot, 2 inches tall at the shoulder
- Weight: 14 - 18 pounds
- Physique: small
- Coat Length: short and smooth
- Skin Texture: soft and silky
- Color: black, fawn, apricot fawn, white,
- Tail: short and curls into its hips
- Temperament: friendly, loyal, jovial, and is happiest when around their caregivers.
- Strangers: will excessively bark at people at the door, most specially strangers
- Children: older children from 11 up.
- Other Pets: gets along well with other with proper socialization and ample time
- Exercise Needs: walking and playing
- Health Conditions: prone to certain canine diseases and health problems
- Lifespan: average 9 to 15 years

Pugs Breed History

This clownish, show-off dog originated from the ancient lands of China and have been documented to join royal ranks of the Han Dynasty as far back as B.C. 206 to A.D. 200. The Pug has established a pretty impressive presence since its introduction to society. Many historians hold the belief that the comical Pug dog is related to the Tibetan Mastiff. Pug dogs were highly priced by the Emperors of China and languished in posh accommodations with soldiers often guarding them.

In the late 1500s and 1600s, the Chinese began trading with European countries. The first Pugs reportedly brought to Europe came with the Dutch traders. They named this breed of Dog from China the Mopshond, and this is a name still used to this day by the locals.

Once they made their appearance in the shores of Europe, they quickly became favorite pets in royal households all across Europe. These loyal beasts are known to have played important roles in the history of many of these royal households. These playful lapdogs became popular Victorian-era subjects and inspirational muses of countless portraits and paintings. The Pugs are illustrated alongside their esteemed royal caregivers, were featured in figurines, and appeared in paintings as well as postcards. Surviving photographs and paintings depict those donning wide, embellished collars, or huge ribbons tied around their thick, short necks. The Pug became the official dog of the House of Orange in Holland after a Pug supposedly saved the life of Prince William, the Prince of Orange. The Pug allegedly gave the Prince a warning that the Spaniards were advancing in 1572.

William of Orange, who was later called William III, along with his wife Mary II, went to England in 1688 to take the throne from James II, and when they did, they had taken along the Pugs with them. At age 15, before marrying Louis XVI, Marie Antoinette owned a Pug she named Mops. Josephine Bonaparte, another famous woman of French and World history, was caregiver to a Pug she had named Fortune. Josephine, before marrying Napoleon Bonaparte was an inmate at the prison in Les Carmes. Her loyal and beloved Pug was the only visitor allowed to see Josephine and the Pug gave way for her to conceal messages in its collar to bring to her family.

The Pugs of England, in the early 1800s, were finally standardized as a breed with two dominant lines. Founded upon the royal canines of Queen Charlotte, spouse of King George III, was the Morrison line. The other line of Pugs was founded on canines imported from Hungary or Russia by the Lord and Lady Willoughby d'Eresby. Two of the pure Chinese lines brought home to England, were named Lamb and Moss. It was the pairing of these two Pugs that bore and birthed Click. Click was a superb canine and was bred countless times to canines from both the Morrison and Willoughby.

To this day, Pugs being a better breed is credited to Click. It was this particular offspring of Moss and Lamb who was instrumental in the overall betterment of Pugs as well as shaping the modern day Pug we know and love today. Concurrently, in China, Pugs were continuously bred by the royal families. When the Chinese Imperial Palace was overrun by the British in 1860, several Pugs were discovered to be under the care of the royal courts and families. Some of the Pugs were brought home to England by the people who were the forerunners of the invasion.

Queen Victoria, who openly fancied Pugs, also bred these canines. Her Royal Majesty greatly favored apricot-fawn Pugs. Another Pug fancier, in the person of Lady Brassey, was responsible for making black Pugs trendy during that era after bringing home some of these black Pugs from China in 1886. It was in 1861 when Pugs were first exhibited to dog aficionados of England. The first volume of the studbook began in 1871 with a record 66 Pugs in registry.

The Many Names of the Pug Dog

The knowledge of existence of black Pugs back in the 1700s is largely owed to the famous English artist and Pug enthusiast, William Hogarth. The artist, with his love for these canines, portrayed a black Pug and many others of its sort in his famous paintings.

The Pug is also portrayed in the paintings of Francisco Goya in the 1780s whilst the painter was in Madrid and under commission as a court painter to the Spanish Crown. Pugs are seen posed and poised beside their caregivers, equally dolled up for the session that would immortalize them on canvass.

Seekers of this canine spread throughout the European regions, as the Pug's popularity rose, it was noted that it was called varied names around Europe, depending on the country on which it had landed. The Pug was called the Dogullo in Spain; the Mops in Germany; the Caganlino in Italy and in France, it was called the Carlin. It was and still is, to this day, called the Mopshand in the Netherlands. Other name the Pug goes by is the Chinese Pug, Dutch bulldog, Dutch mastiff and Mini mastiff.

Chapter Two: Requirements of Pugs

Knowing what your new Pug dog needs in terms of food, lodging, care, grooming, exercise, play, medical care and activities are important details a potential caregiver must know. The care and rearing of a puppy does not end after acquisition - in fact, it is just the start. Building a relationship with your Pug will be one of the most rewarding experiences you will cherish in life. Start off the new union by reading up extensively on the traits and personality as well as the needs and requirements of your a Pug dog to aid in its successful integration to its new family.

In this chapter you will find useful information that will provide you a clear idea of what your Pug will need to enjoy a life of happy contentment at home.

Pros and Cons of Owning a Pug

The pros and cons of taking in a Pug are some considerations you will want to ponder before making the decision of adding one to the family dynamics. Noteworthy traits of the Pug are oftentimes described as clownish and playful, other times said to be dignified and tranquil, constantly lauded as stable and sturdy, as well as consistently amiable and good humored.

The Pug will have a lot to say with its odd sounding bark when strangers and visitors arrive at your doorstep. It will then welcome the newcomer, if allowed into the portals of your home, with snuffles, grunts, and snorts. Though they are fine when in the midst of other pets and animals, Pugs can get very jealous if it sees another pet occupying your lap. As stubborn as they may seem at times, the stable Pug will rarely get into any real mischief. Mature Pugs will spend most of the day in dreamland, asleep. Housebreaking your Pug can be a bit of a challenge especially when it rains. Another embarrassing problem they have is their shameless tendency to release gas.

Pros:

Should you desire a canine who…
- is small, yet blocky and stocky
- has large expressive eyes set on a short, snub face
- is generally polite with everyone, including other animals, pets and children
- does not need too much exercise
- seldom gets into mischief

Cons

If do not want to deal with…

- snuffling, snorting, snoring, wheezing and occasional slobbering
- flatulence (gas)
- challenges in housebreaking
- daily shedding as a constant
- a few potential health issues due to his deformed face

The good news is, the cons listed here are avoidable and can be minimized by dealing with a reputable breeder who will hand over a healthy puppy into your expectant arms. Training your dog to give you respect is another way to stave off the ill behaviors perceived in the Pug.

Letting the Pug know early in its life that the alpha is around the house will need discipline and consistency from you.

Alternatively, you can do a good deed by adopting an adult Pug from your local rescue group or animal shelter. Rescuing a canine from a shelter, proven to be free of negative traits and most likely housebroken, will not only cost much less - you would have also saved a canine from a certain and unfortunate fate. Personnel from the shelter may not have concrete answers or documentation for the Pug so be aware that you may potentially be bringing home a Pug with existing medical conditions.

License Requirements

Attending to the business of acquiring a license for your Pug is a law requirement that you will have to factor into the yearly expenses of your Pug. A license is required across states and will be necessary for identification purposes should animal control happen to chance upon a "loitering" canine.

The annual license fee costs anywhere from $10-$20. By default, animals that have not been spayed or neutered have to pay higher fees as opposed to animals that they have undergone the de-sexing procedure. The rationale for the raised fees for unaltered animals is to encourage caregivers to get their pets "fixed". In some places like King County, Washington, license for an unaltered animal will cost $60 - the good news is, caregivers are given a $25 voucher which is accepted by many local vets and can go toward payment for the procedure.

Cost Cutting Methods

Licenses for signal, service and trained guide dogs who are employed to assist their disabled caregivers are usually free. Sometimes, older people or disabled individuals are provided free licenses which have undergone alteration. Other cities also give a little reprieve to caregivers whose household income fall below a certain amount. Micro-chipped or tattooed canines in Pennsylvania are able to obtain lifetime licenses due to their identification chip. Being caregiver to many canines may require a kennel license which will cover all the canines under your care.

Counties and city governments are regulators of animals within their jurisdiction. A caregiver will usually be able to get their license in the mail and others can be provided online. Let your fingers do the walking and look for the licensing department of your city or county in the phonebook.

Most states will require a caregiver to submit a certificate of current rabies vaccination in order to obtain a dog license. This is why puppies are exempt from having a license until they are of the proper rabies vaccination age of about 4 months old. Local governments maintain transparency between them and canine caregivers by way of a canine's vaccination records; the administering vet is bound by law to send a record to the county reflecting whether or not a dog is licensed.

Towns offering reduced license fees will require you to show proof of eligibility such as a vet certificate indicating that the canine has been spayed or neutered; or a certificate from a canine training institute reflecting that the canine is a trained guide dog.

Relocation from an issuing city or country will almost certainly entail getting a new one from the location to which you are moving. There are a few states, like New Jersey, where a license is recognized anywhere within the state. Moving out of state will most definitely need a guardian to apply for and purchase another license from that state within a 30-day span upon arrival in the new state

Not purchasing a canine license for your dog can be likened to driving a car without one. If you do not break road rules, get stopped by a police, or hit another vehicle then no one will be the wiser. So if your Pug is never lost, nabbed by animal control, bothers the neighbors, stolen, or bite anyone you could try to do away with it. However, if any of these situations occur, the fine for absence of dog license will be a lot steeper and costlier than going through the necessary procedures of getting one from the onset.

Licensed canines nabbed and impounded by animal control personnel run through the system to identify locate and notify the canine's caregiver of the incident. On the other hand, the fate of unlicensed dogs is much bleaker and even grim - unlicensed dogs which are unsuccessfully reunited with their guardians are euthanized sooner than licensed ones. The two-three days a licensed dog is given at the facilities could mean the difference between getting it back and permanently losing it.

Behavior with Children and Pets

Pugs are big fans of children and adore the attention it gets whilst around them. They may be small but do not be deceived of their size; they are hardly what you would call delicate as some other toy breeds are. This robust nature of the Pug makes it a perfect candidate for families with older children who extend kindness and loving attention toward it.

As leader of the pack and responsible caregiver of the canine, you should inform the younger people in the home of the inherent traits of the Pug so as not to set lofty expectations of the puppy's abilities. You could try to teach it tricks but do not be frustrated at the seeming indifference of Pugs, as they are not great retrievers of balls and certainly not fond of kicking one around either. If a Pug is trained well and is socialized early in its life, the Pug will enjoy and appreciate the company of other canines. Most Pugs have been observed to be a feline-friendly dogs that will extend kindness and patience to an existing feline pet given patience, time and space for successful integration.

Keep in mind that adult caregivers must consistently supervise all initial interactions of the new Pug when in the presence of children and other pets. This safety measure of supervision is recommended so that playtime does not get out of hand and no players get carried away.

Initial Costs

Determining the financial implications of a new pet is an important monetary detail you will want to figure out very early on as you ponder the inclusion of a Pug to your family. You will need to first seek out a breeder of good repute to deal with because as mentioned earlier, the history of the pups' parents will be vital information which will give you an idea of the overall health of the pup.

A Pug will cost anywhere from $400 - $2000 and will hinge on factors like, availability of history, quality of dog, as well as location from which it will originate, if the canine is bought out of state or country. The price of the Pug will also largely depend on whether the Pug is of pet quality or of show quality with the latter costing much more than the former.

No matter what amount you pay for your pet quality canine, keep in mind that you should be furnished with the Pugs medical records. It should have been given all its puppy shots and must have been de-wormed with at least a one year health guarantee. The next thing to prepare for would be shipping costs of the canine if it is coming from out of state or country. The best way to determine this cost is to get in touch with shippers to find out the specifics of handling as well as the final cost of shipping.

You will need to purchase equipment your Pug will need once it is ready to be taken home. A sturdy crate can cost anywhere from $50 - $250 and will be routinely used by you and your Pug for trips outside the home.

You will also need to get feeding and drinking dishes. You will want to avoid exposure to any toxic chemicals or materials which may make your Pug sick; stainless steel or ceramic feeders are some sound choices to consider. Not only do they last longer, they are also free from toxins and chemicals used in the production of less desirable feeding implement choices.

Here is a short list of initial expenses you are looking at which will give you an idea if you are financially able to take in a Pug:

- Food and Treats - $300 to $700
- Toys - $50 to $150
- Harness - $25 to $75
- Grooming (Supplies or Professional Grooming) - $75 to $500
- Veterinarian (Shots, De-worming, Checkups, Health Issues) - $200 to $1000
- Medications (Heartworm, etc. and Supplements) - $100 to $300
- Yearly Total: $750 to $2725
- Monthly Expense: $62 to $227

Can a Pug Be Left Alone?

Separation anxiety is a very real struggle your Pug experiences when it is left home alone. Do not mistake her barking, yapping and complaints as bad behavior because this is your Pugs way of expressing herself faced with an emotional situation it is not prepared or equipped to handle.

Guardians will need to step out of the house to earn a living, run errands, attend social events and more often than not won't be able to bring their Pug along for these short forays outside the house. Identifying anxiety in your Pug is important because you will, at a very early stage, have to teach your Pug to cope with stretches of time by herself without falling depressed. Having to suffer through stress on a daily basis can definitely take a physical toll on anyone, and this is a reality many Pugs live through.

You will not be able to see what your Pug goes through when you are at work, so it will be difficult to determine its reality unless your home is outfitted with security-monitoring cameras with which you can use to virtually peek into your home and Pug.

In lieu of expensive home-spyware, your diligent observation will help you recognize your Pugs behavior as you ready yourself for the day. Your loyal Pug will begin to sense a shift in your demeanor as you rush about doing a hundred things morning's demand of you. Be reminded that the Pug is a sensitive dog that is in sync with your moods and emotions. Therefore as you are flooded by harried emotions and hounded by impending tasks at this time of the day, so your Pug is too. As tempting as it is to fall back on the habit of the running-like-a-headless-chicken syndrome, don't.

Help your Pug by making separation painless and fuss-free. Experiment with different methods to calm her and stick with the one she responds to positively. You can start by making time for quality one-on-one with your Pug in the mornings. Wake up a little earlier than you usually do to talk to and spend time with your Pug. Your discipline in observing consistency at this stage is essential. Unwavering consistency will reap you positive results in the long run and will save your sweet Pug from feeling lonesome whilst you are away.

You want to create a relaxed atmosphere for your Pug to ward off any feelings of foreboding; in time you will note an air of confidence in your dog even when faced with your imminent departure. Provide your Pug with a safe haven and a comfortable space which she associates with you and where he can feel safe. To do this use an indoor pen and equip it will all the neat, fun things she and you enjoy. Figure out whether your dog prefers being close to a window, where it can peer out into the world, or if it would rather not be reminded of what it is missing stuck indoors and adjust pen to canine's preference.

Keep the pen doors open when you are at home, tidy up as you talk softly and lovingly to it. Give it a gentle nudge to stay in its bed if it seems sleepy - the goal is to make your Pug understand that this is her special space, her "den". Keep the space clean and furnished with all her favorite playthings; sound-emitting chew toys, treat-release toys, and an array of its own stuffed-animal toys.

Do not under any circumstance; leave your Pug inside her crate. This will be very confusing for your Pug, especially if you utilize the crate to bring it on trips. Imagine getting all riled up and excited for a road trip with you only to be left in confusion as you step out without it. The Pug will not thrive caged in like this and may likely develop behavioral problems due to the very restricted space of a crate. She will likely make more of a ruckus and forget all manners due to daily confinement.

What are the Pros and Cons of Pugs?

Before choosing a pet, it is important that you get to know them better first. Every dog is different, every breed is unique. That is the reason why it is important to get to know them first by doing some research. This can help you decided whether a certain breed is suitable for you. This section contains a list of pros and cons in having a Pug dog. This can help you determine whether this breed fits you well.

Pros for Pug Dogs

Get this type of breed…

- If you are not a first time dog owner and you have a lot of patience in training dogs
- If you can handle an energetic dog
- If you want a dependable watch dog, bit at the same time sociable around strangers
- If you want a medium-sized dog

Cons for Pug Dogs

- They are challenging to train at first
- They have a very dynamic temperament which makes them hard to handle if not properly trained
- They like digging holes and destroying things if they are not properly house trained.
- They constantly shed and can leave a lot of hair all over the place
- They can be aggressive towards other dogs and pets
- They bark excessively

Chapter Three: Tips on Buying Pug Dogs

Whilst on the quest of finding your Pug dog, a potential caregiver has to be aware of important factors that will spell the success or failure of the canine's integration to its new home and family. The temperament of a Pug is influenced by a number of factors which includes heredity, training methods, food it is fed and how early or late it is introduced to social situations.

Puppies who are even-tempered are playful, curious, are not shy to approach people. They welcome the interaction, happy to be cuddled, petted and held by humans. Observe the puppies individually and choose one who displays middle-of-the-road characteristics; one who does not cower in a corner, does not bully and beat up on his siblings or littermates. Meeting the parents of the puppy, usually the dam or mother of the offspring will give indication of the personality of the pup. Meeting relatives of the dam and sire as well as its siblings is helpful when evaluating what a puppy may be like when it matures.

Finding a Reputable Breeder

Just like other pedigreed canines, Pugs are to be produced utilizing ethical methods. This is to minimize the likelihood of the Pug inheriting medical conditions this particular canine is prone to if bred in a manner without thought or consideration. Adding a pet to your home is not as simple or carefree as it seems. Acquisition of one requires, thoughtful care, knowledge of the canine's strengths and weaknesses, patience, love, time and of course, money. Being properly knowledgeable of all these details will allow you to nurture your new pet in a suitable, happy home environment.

Finding the right breeder to partner up with will be one of the most important tasks you shall have to be extremely mindful of. You will want to research the credibility, the success rate and methods employed by this very important player in your quest to have a Pug join your family. Now will be a good time to start networking with seasoned Pug owners to find out if they can give you helpful tips to breeders with whom you could do business. You may also ask your vet for breeder recommendations as they may quite likely be able to point you to a successful one.

Upstanding Pug breeders will be able to furnish you will information pertinent to the pup whilst allowing you to be a part of every step of the breeding process. The amount you pay for the puppy can be an indicator of the attention and care extended to the young canine. A reputable breeder will assure you and even guarantee that only ethical methods are practiced during the process. Given that you only work with an upstanding breeder and all goes as it should, you can expect to welcome a healthy, happy, even-tempered pup who has been given initial inoculation and proper vet attention.

You will want to deal with breeders who are transparent with their breeding methods and are open to welcoming you to their facilities. Witnessing the interaction between facility administrators and the puppies within their premises will allow you to see how the animals are treated and cared for whilst there. It will also allow you to meet the canine mother and father the breeders will be using to produce your Pug. These breeders will be in the position to furnish you the history and medical background of both the parents backed up with documentation.

A breeder of good intentions and upstanding repute will not only be able to answer a slew of questions you throw at them, they will equally be happy to offer and impart information which they understand will be important details for you to know. Breeders of this stature will also have questions to ask potential guardians to help them identify if the home the dog will be joining is a suitable one. On the other hand, breeders who give shady answers, refuses to give you access to their facilities or makes excuses to stave off a likely visit from a future guardian is to be struck out of the list of breeders.

Selecting a Healthy and Even-Tempered Pug Pup

When selecting a Pug pup a good rule of thumb to follow is to choose the puppy best suited for you. Whatever you do, do not be carried away by the expressive eyes of the Pug and have the canine choose you. Well-meaning friends may advise you to pick the one who runs right up to you and eagerly wags its tail at the sight of you. However, this only results in the boldest and pushiest puppies to be chosen above all. Gentler puppies that politely wait their turn for attention may be pushed to the background and completely ignored in the process of picking. Make it your resolve to get to know each puppy and give them all a fair shake before making a decision.

Pugs may present themselves as something likeable, this may be amusing and cute at the beginning but may pose to be problematic later when you need to integrate the Pug dog into your home. You may discover that the readily sociable ones are the one who are more likely to be difficult to train later. On the other hand, a shy pup could equally be difficult to deal with especially if the trait of shyness is hardwired into its genes. A shy pup will grow up to be a shy adult who can be act defensively if frightened or startled.

Normal puppies are trusting, curious, and friendly. They would gather at your feet, pull on your shoelaces, nibble on your digits, crawl onto your lap, and usually would be on a quest to check out each and every little thing. You will be able to learn something about the individual personality of a pup by seeing how they relate toward their littermates. Determining which ones are strong, bossy, outgoing, quiet, submissive, gentle, and which ones grab at toys will give you an idea of their temperament and individual traits. You will be able to determine all these by observation and will eventually help you conclude which ones in the litter are delicate and which ones are more stubborn than the rest.

Once you finish evaluating the whole lot you will want to observe each canine in its natural surroundings when away from the rest of the litter. This is after all what the situation will be when you bring home your Pug. Observe for major shifts in its actions and disposition when away from the rest. This will give you an idea of how the Pug will be once separated from its parents and siblings when taken home. Make it a point to get to know the unique personality of your soon-to-be Pug and it will save you from unexpected surprises. You will be able to determine if the Pug will get along well with the rest of the family.

Chapter Four: Maintenance for Pugs

At this point of your research, you are closer to knowing more about the lovable Pug and what to expect when you take in and live with one. It will be up to you and other adult caregivers who will be sharing responsibility for the new Pug to know what to provide the canine. Outfit your home and make sure that your new Pug comes home to a safe haven which has been dog-proofed, not only for its safety but also for the general safety of everyone with whom it will share space and abode.

Keep in mind that taking in a pet is a responsibility not to be taken lightly. They will highly depend on you for their everyday requirements of attention, care, food and affection. Knowing what to do in the event of emergencies and unforeseen situations will be on your shoulders. Being able to recognize signs of discomfort and changes in your dog's everyday routine or habits will help you determine if they are in need of medical assistance.

The responsibility of being Pug guardian is a job that should not to be taken lightly. Yes, your Pug will thrive as long as its guardians and caregivers carry out their duties to the tiny, furry canine. With that said, Pugs will still require basic sundries to keep them healthy, happy, and engaged.

This section of the book aims to give you time tested recommendations that will ensure a Pugs contentment whilst under your loving care.

Tips on Dog-Proofing Your Home

Remember that one factor to keeping your dog happy is to provide it with an environment where it is safe. As you make provisions for the new Pug take thoughtful, calculated measures when preparing your home and yard for your new canine's arrival and remove any possible dangers.

The natural curiosity of canine shows up when they are in strange surroundings, they will want to get their noses into every little nook and cranny of a new space with no regard for its safety. All it is focused on is its quest for discovery. It will be up to you to outfit and refit your home to meet a certain level of security so that your dog is safe during its exploration.

Make your home a safe environment for your new pet. Not only will mindful preparation benefit your new canine, it will also afford you some peace of mind that you have done all which is necessary to make your home a safe haven for all.

Bathrooms and Kitchens

These areas of the home contain a number of hazards that if your Pug went into, could cause it harm or pose grave danger to its safety.

Cleaning products, hair products, medication and pharmaceuticals are items comprised mostly of very toxic substances that are very dangerous to pets if they come into contact with these. For your peace of mind and to help maintain organization of your home, do the necessary to keep your inquisitive canine away from these items.

- Store all cleaning agents, laundry and bath soaps, shampoos, fabric softeners of all sorts and kinds, away from where your Pug's curiosity could get the better of it. Make an investment and install child-proof locks on your cabinet doors. This will not only keep your prying Pug from these poisonous items - keeping cabinet doors closed and locked discourages your tiny lapdog from crawling into spaces where it may not be noticed.

- Keep all kinds of food out of your pets reach by securing food containers with tight, air-proof jars. Keep unused food in the pantry or in the refrigerator. You will not only discourage scrounging for food you will also save yourself the work of cleaning up a mess created by your little buddy's curiosity.

- Securely fasten all garbage bins with tight covers. Secure lids will not only keep litter in the bin, it will also keep your nosey little buddy out of a smelly mess.

- Make certain that all laundry hatches, washer and dryer doors are closed and fastened. Your Pug is one who enjoys the escape of dreamland and will sometimes retreat to quiet places where it can curl up and snooze. You will want to check the insides of these places before using them should you forget to close them.

- Keep toilet lids closed at all times. The possibility of your Pug taking a drink of water from a bowl laden with chemicals will be very toxic and harmful for your dog. Another danger an open toilet bowl poses is the possibility of your Pug falling into it. This can be a difficult situation for your Pug pup to get out of on occasion when it is on its own.

- To dissuade your Pug from crawling into small spaces it may have difficulty getting out of, cover and block spaces your Pug will likely investigate and could end up getting trapped.

Living Area

The living room seems like a safe enough area since this is the common room where the family gathers. Since your eventual addition will be more likely to get into places than the rest of the family, you will want to take caution and reassess your living room space.

- If you have indoor plants, you will first want to determine if these plants are non-toxic to your canine. Toxic poisoning from ingesting plants is a very real possibility. You will want to remove these plants from the general area where your Pug is given freedom to roam. Not only to keep them from tipping one over and creating a mess, but more so to avoid an avoidable trip to the vet.

- Cover all heating and air vents.

- Remove or protect with plastic wire covering all string, ropes, wires and electric cables. Loose string and rope may entangle your little Pug and cause it distress and worse. Electrical wires, if played with or chewed on can cause a nasty electric shock to your Pug.

- Curios, souvenirs, fragile mementos and breakable valuables should be stored away or placed in another room and out of the Pugs line of sight or reach. Avoid accidents that may happen should the Pug get too close for comfort.

- Use a box to store away toys used during play. Toys with small parts or are easily breakable and pose a choking hazard to toddlers and your Pug.

Rooms

- Cosmetics, medicine, liquids in jars and tubes, keys, jewelry, pills, and other small items your Pug can reach and handle are curiosities which he may gravitate to when in the exploring mood. Save yourself the trouble of cleaning up after your curious buddy, and the dread of learning it had swallowed something it isn't supposed to swallow.

- As with the wires in the living room, make sure that you use the same protective coverings on any exposed wires to dissuade your Pug from chewing on a live wire. Cover any sockets that are unused for extra measure.

- Keep cabinet doors closed so that your Pug doesn't crawl into it without being noticed. Nothing raises stress levels than calling out for an animal hidden in an unsecured nook, oblivious to the world around it and fast asleep.

Backyard and Garage

These are possibly some of the more dangerous spots for your Pug should you allow it to wander off into these areas of the house. Should your Pug have to spend time by itself whilst you are at work, it will be sound to check and recheck for hazards it could come across.

- Take stock of the supplies you store in the garage. All paints, cleaning agents, tools, gas cans, etc., should be stored away from its sight and secured by doors with child-proof locks.

- Make sure that you do not leave out supplies and materials you use for a project. Take stock that all tools and implements are stored and locked away.

- Your Pug is small. It will get into places that it may not be able to get out of on its own. Cover all possible crawl spaces for an extra measure of peace.

- Check fences for holes your frolic Pug may wiggle through. Not only could it hurt itself as it forces its body through the gap, it is also a gateway for the Pug to get out of and away from the safety of its home.

- Before driving off, check that the dog did not crawl under the car, this scenario is an all too real one and has caused heartbreaks many times over. Before leaving, conduct a pet headcount. Call out loudly to your Pug and honk the horn to make sure it hasn't camped out under the car.

Environmental Requirements for Your Pug

Your playful Pug will need its own space to move in and about most specially if it is to be left alone for a good portion of the day. Giving it a fenced off area where it can play, sleep and eat independently will help it get used to periodic solitude.

Make sure there are no breakable items within its reach which it may tip over and shatter whilst you are away. Store away all cherished mementos, souvenirs, gifts and knick knacks that may shatter in shards and hurt the canine whilst you are away. Most plants are toxic to dogs so make sure that you research existing plants in and around your home to find out if these are safe for the new addition in your home. Should you determine the presence of toxic foliage in and around your home, make an effort to either plant them farther away from the area your dog is allowed to wander or, better yet, replace them with dog-friendly plants.

You will want to dog-proof each room your canine is allowed to roam. Mount sturdy child-proof locks to fasten cabinet doors which contain cleaning agents, bathroom supplies, and medicine - all of which can make your canine ill or worse. Store and stash away other small objects which, if discovered and played with by your Pug, could be ingested and lodged in your her system.

In these modern days of advanced technology and our apparent never ending quest of gadget upgrades, wires run aplenty. Save yourself, someone else and your pets the jarring shock of electrocution. Take care that there are no exposed electrical wires which may cause a nasty shock and cover visible wires in the room with plastic guards. Mind that strings from blinds or drapery ropes are out of your playful dogs reach as this may cause them to accidentally entangle themselves whilst at play.

Make sure that garbage bins are tightly fitted with lids that will not come off in the event it is tipped over. Another thing you will want to make a habit of is closing the lids of toilets when not in use lest the canine wanders into the toilet and attempts to drink out of the bowl. Falling into an uncovered toilet bowl is also a very real situation your Pug could experience and cause it grave distress if no one is there to give it immediate assistance.

Keep all medicines high up and stored away in child-proofed cabinets which are out of the reach of your Pug. Medicines, vitamins and supplements meant for human use are highly dangerous if ingested by your young pup. Save him from the discomfort, adverse effects and an untimely visit to the vet.

Toys and Sundries for Your Buddy

Providing toys to entertain and engage your Pug will not just help him to develop his abilities and talents, these toys will also be essential boredom-busters which will keep him busy. Make sure that the toys you purchase for your dog are items that will keep him company and occupied for the times when he is left alone. Many owners make the mistake of buying on impulse because an item looks cute or is on sale. Choose wisely when purchasing toys and pick the ones which will aid in the independent play and chewing needs of the canine.

Dogs have an innate and natural need to chew on something constantly. Teething and chew toys are perfect for younger puppies that will need to find some relief when its gums are sore during the teething phase. Find chew toys that have cooling properties which can offer relief during this difficult time of teething. Some chew toys have cooling gels which offer relief and have properties which allow it to freeze faster when placed in the freezer. Be sure to double up on this conveniently soothing toy whilst your little buddy is teething.

Boredom is a real situation your Pug will go through if not engaged with the proper tools to keep it entertained. Other toy choices you will want to bring home to your Pug are toys that speak or move about. There are many of these sorts of toys available in the market and you will definitely want to invest in a durable one for your adorable Pug. Many of these toys were specifically fashioned to engage, interact, keep pets company and even soothe them. This will be a worthwhile purchase which will provide your furry pal hours of entertainment.

Remember that Pugs do not do well alone and will suffer from separation anxiety if not properly provided with the right kind of toys to keep it distracted and engaged. The advances in technology have exponentially improved and only continue to get better. A popular pet toy available today is one which emits warmth and a soothing heartbeat meant to mimic the presence of another living creature. These toys can be used to bring your Pug comfort and a sense of relief whilst the guardian is out of the house. Pugs can cuddle up to these toys and feel a sense of acknowledgement and the warmth of another "buddy" present.

There are also toys that a guardian can teach the Pug to use. These toys will release treats and rewards when operated correctly. Not only can this toy reaffirm and build confidence in the dog through mental stimulation it will also help build up confidence as it gives the Pug a rewarding sense of accomplishment.

Be sure that you regularly clean these toys to avoid bacterial contamination. If your Pug shows favor toward a utilitarian toy is sure to double up and get a backup for when the old one needs to be retired. Aim for quality over quantity when toy shopping for your Pug and inspect the toys regularly for wear and tear; a damaged toy may come apart during play and may end up being ingested and lodged in the bowel tracks of your Pug.

A Pug will only need about 6 - 8 pieces of toys and no more than that. Your job will be to seek out the proper sort of toys which will engage, entertain and keep your Pug company. Take heed in choosing the right kind of toys for your Pug as they will not need too many, but will definitely need the right ones to ward off any feelings of anxiety.

Tips in Keeping Your Pug Happy Indoors and Outdoors

Incomplete information and misinformation about caring for canines are aplenty on the Internet and spread through word of mouth. Although well-meaning in intention, outdated or partial information, if mistakenly taken to heart and followed can run the risk of your canine living a shorter, unhealthier existence.

Raising your Pug on misinformation or partial and selected knowledge can hinder its overall wellbeing and successful growth. Here are some tips to keep your new Pug in the pink of health and happily content inside and outside the homestead.

A potential guardian needs to know that the wrong kinds of food can lead to chronic health issues that could plague your Pug all through its life. You might never think of associating excessive shedding, loose stools, ear infections, and flatulence to the food you are feeding it, but remember that the health of your Pug will begin with the quality of food it is fed. You can read up more on what types of food you can feed your Pug in chapter five.

The wrong vaccinations and too many of them at a time will not only make your Pug horribly ill, but will also weaken the immune system of your loyal canine, leaving it more susceptible to illnesses. Applying the wrong anti-flea products, even those labeled as "natural" can be toxic to your Pug. When neutered or spayed at the wrong age, a Pug can experience and suffer from bladder control issues - also known as incontinence - later in its life.

Giving it the wrong chew toys can cause your Pug to suffer from diarrhea, intestinal blockage, choking, vomiting or even death.

Bringing your dog to the wrong vet may mean an unhappy lifetime of ingesting medications, drugs and chemicals for your Pug with all the side effects to boot. You would never entrust the life and health of a beloved member of the family to an unreliable health practitioner so make sure that your vet is one who takes great pride in their calling and extends only the strictest professional health care your Pug deserves.

Chapter Five: Nutritional Needs of Pug Dogs

The health and overall future well-being of your new Pug will depend highly on the quality of food you provide it. You, as caregiver, carry the task of selecting the right sort of food which will supply your Pug all the essential nutrients it needs to live a happy life. Expect to experiment with different foods at the beginning until you figure out which nutritionally sound brand your Pug likes best before buying in bulk.

Unlike times in the past when pet foods were few to choose from options are unlimited these days. With such an extensive selection to choose from, the task of picking out the right kinds of food for your Pug can be a daunting one if you do not know what your Pug needs and what to avoid.

This would be a good time to educate yourself about the many ways manufacturers label their foods and how these labels give way to identifying what foods, additives and other whatnots manufacturers put into their food mixes to produce their products.

Ask your vet about raw and home feeding if you choose to go this route. Knowing the exact needs of your Pug dog is important to know as you will have a more active and participative role in the purchase, quality control, preparation and measurement of the meals you will be giving it.

Types of Commercial Food Brands

As you research further into finding out what foods to feed, and not feed, your Pug you will come across a lot of marketing hype which you will want to ignore. Learning to read and decipher labels and what ingredients, additives and extenders go into the mix is a skill you will want to develop.

Store brought brands, in order to give their product volume and flavor use extenders like soy and corn which serve no nutritional value to your dog and may cause allergies. Many of these pet foods also contain meat by-products, which are the unused parts and rejected portions of an animal previously processed for the consumption of humans like, cow hoof, pig nose, fatty and bony parts of chicken, face, ears and shockingly, even road kill.

Toxic Foods to Avoid

The saying that 'everything in moderation' is not to be applied to the Pug's diet! There are a number of specific foods your Pug will adversely react to. Do your Pug a solid and learn up on what sort of foods they are not supposed to have which make them painfully sick or gravely ill.

It should go without saying that any sort of alcohol isn't good for your Pug pet. However many caregivers have thought it amusing to see their Pugs lap up the intoxicating liquid. Alcohol poisoning is nothing to laugh about.

Onions and garlic are ingredients popularly used in preparation of human foods. Too much of these spices ingested by your Pug will negatively affect the red blood cell count of your Pug.

The cooked bones of rabbit and chicken pose threat to your dog's stomach because they break and splinter. These could potentially cause intestinal perforations and blockages as well as tongue lacerations and broken teeth.

Baking soda can cause congestive heart failure and muscle spasms so watch that your Pug isn't getting his little face into your baked goods. Coffee products are also very toxic substances which affect your Pugs heart and nervous system. Caffeine also causes vomiting, seizures, tremors, irregular and increased heart rate, fever, diarrhea, coma and even death. All sorts of chocolates pose potential dangers to your Pug, some more than others; reactions to the adverse effects of chocolate on your Pug may not manifest until a day after ingestion. Do not attempt to give your Pug a corncob to chew on because these are not digested by your buddy and may become lodged in his intestinal track.

Avocadoes are definitely foods not for your Pug as they have fungicidal toxin that when ingested can lead to an inflammation of your buddy's pancreas. Other fruits to avoid altogether would be raisins, currants and grapes because they contain toxins which damage your Pugs kidneys.

Keep pits of cherries, plums, apricots and peaches away from 'reach and out of your dog's mouth - at all costs! The pits contain cyanogen glycosides, which can result in cyanide poisoning. Instead, slice off a portion of the fruit and give it to your Pug.

Keep in mind that you will need to study up on and conduct proper research to discover other foods that your Pug may react adversely toward. Talk with your breeder and consult with your vet to get a clearer idea of other foods may be dangerous to your Pug's health. It will be largely up to you to find out which foods to avoid so as keeping your Pug happily in the pink of health.

Tips in Selecting High-Quality Dog Food

Networking with a small circle of experienced Pug owners, breeders and health providers has been mentioned within this book a number of times for good reason. Having a close set of 'advisers' allows the sharing of best practices, pet food recipes, commercial food choices, and a world of useful information for the novice Pug guardian.

Be an informed, smart and thorough shopper and learn to decipher complicated ingredient names found on manufacturers labels. Understand the truth behind labels which read 'meat by-product', 'by-products' or 'meal' because these are in fact what was mentioned earlier in the previous bit to be remains and odd parts of previously processed animal.

Canned pet foods are made to be tasty to a canine's palate, easy to store, and have very little preservatives. This is why canned foods are to be consumed immediately after serving or it will go bad. Canned pet foods are costlier than pet foods but are a perfect choice for very young pups or a much older canine. It will contain a higher concentration of water so the canine will probably need a bigger serving if this is on the menu.

Pet foods which are semi-moist are chewier in consistency and are stored in bags of varied weights. Compared to dry foods, semi-moist foods enjoy a shorter shelf life. These foods also contain sugar, to maintain the soft density of the food. These frequently also have food coloring making the food appear more appealing. Some canines have been noted to experience challenges metabolizing these products resulting in softer more frequent bowel movements. This sort of food is not recommended to be given as main meals but rather as treats.

Another choice in the pet food spectrum is the least expensive of all; commercially produced dry foods or kibble. These foods, which enjoys a longer shelf life in comparison to wet or semi-moist canine foods, has been said to help stave off the buildup of plaque and tar in the canine's teeth. You will need to employ your sleuthing skills to understand the labels on packages as many of the dry foods contain additives which have no nutritional value to your Pug. Remember that you will find an endless selection of pet food products to choose from, some better than others.

Home cooked meals and raw feeding are alternative options you may want to consider if feeling overwhelmed by the many choices. Consult with your vet if you choose to feed your canine raw or home cooked food as you will have to measure out other ingredients to complete a balanced dish each time.

How (Often) To Feed Your Pug Dogs

Your Pug will always seem to want more food and it will most likely try anything and everything you offer it. It will even get into food not offered it if food were left out where your voraciously keen eater may reach. A potential guardian is warned to monitor what foods are given the Pug to avoid obesity.

Free feeding your Pug is only recommended when it is young; until it is 3 months old. From the time your Pug first has her first solid meal until it is 3 months old, free feeding is acceptable to help it gain weight. This is also the best time to figure out the sort of foods your Pug responds to with eagerness. As you move toward the fourth month of solid foods, lessen the frequency of the feeding to 3 measured meals, given at consistent times of the day. Feeding outside of a schedule will contradict and throw off house training your Pug.

Remember that teaching and instilling discipline at an early age, in all areas of your Pug's life, is essential to a successful home life. Not only will disciplined feeding, grooming, and outdoor time help you factor all these into your weekly and daily schedule, it will also have your canine be raised in a home where consistency is observed - resulting in a more socialized and even-mannered companion. A Pug aged a year and over is ideally given 2 measured meals a day at specific, determined times of the day.

Chapter Six: Caring Guidelines for Pug dogs

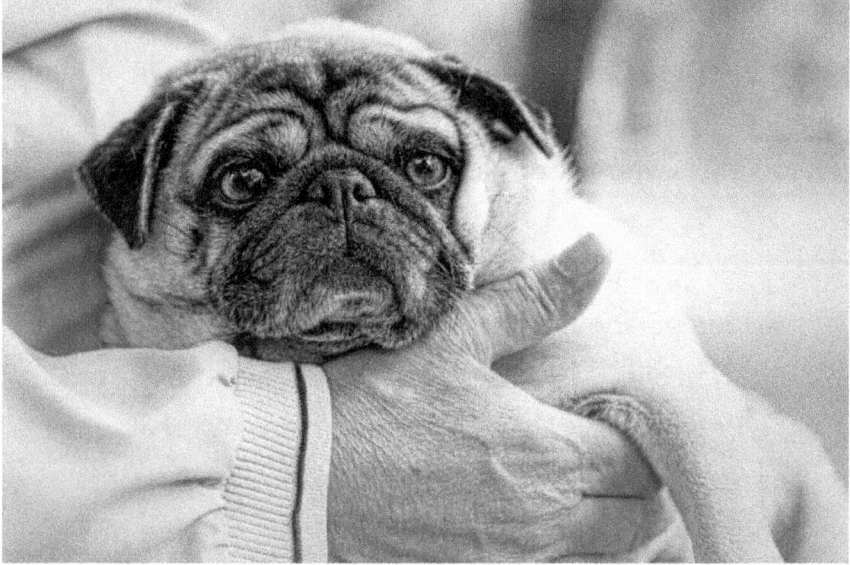

The Pug is a playfully social canine who will gladly receive attention from people it meets and comes across. It is important for a future guardian to determine which situations and environments a Pug will best thrive in.

The task of caring for your new Pug addition will largely fall on the shoulders of responsible caregivers in the family. It is but sound for the each of the family members - most especially those who will be taking on these obligations to research, study and learn what they can do to assist in bringing out the best talents and abilities of the Pug.

Socializing and Training Your Pug

Early socialization is highly recommended for any pet a potential guardian wants to take into their fold. Exposing the canine early to various social situations, like meeting different people helps the puppy develop social manners at an early age and puts you at an advantage in terms of raising a well-rounded, well-mannered, socialized Pug.

Your diligence and patience in exposing the Pug to various personalities you deal with regularly; its exposure to different sights, sounds, surroundings and experiences helps the Pug develop an even temperament. A great way to start off the socialization of your Pug is by enrolling it in a kindergarten puppy class. Be sure that you are present for these training classes as these classes will also teach you many things to effectively handle situations you may encounter with your Pug when the trainer is not present. Your presence will also ensure that you are aware of the skills your Pug has learnt as well as its progress. A potential caregiver will benefit greatly during this most opportune period of training when both caregiver and canine learn commands.

Minimizing Health Problems

Minimize the problems your Pug may go through and commit to taking extra steps to keeping your Pug healthy. Here are some medical conditions a Pug is prone to which you will want to discuss in detail with your vet should you have any concerns. The respiratory of the Pug is compromised so it is strongly advised that smokers refrain from smoking around the Pug. Keep the canine away from allergenic pollen and freshly pruned foliage. Do not use strong chemical products to clean and opt for the more neutral and natural choices.

If your Pug needs to undergo anesthesia, make certain your vet only employs the most modern anesthetics such as isoflurane, and strongly insist on a blood pressure and heart monitor. There are many vets who are not thoughtful or mindful when administering anesthesia to animals, specially short-faced breeds like your Pug. It will be up to you to research, ask questions and ultimately refuse anything that will be dangerous to your Pugs life.

Minimize outdoor activities during hot or humid weather and keep him comfortably indoors in an environment of regulated air-conditioning. Short-faced canines run a higher risk of suffering from heatstroke because they may not able to pant vigorously to lower their body temperature on their own.

If you need to employ a leash when walking your Pug, opt instead for a Y-shaped harness which will wrap around the Pugs chest instead of its throat. A collar wrapped around its neck makes it harder for the Pug to breathe as this puts pressure on its windpipe. Make it a habit to thoroughly and completely wash and dry the folds of the Pugs face after each meal as the wrinkly skin of the Pug may become irritated with rash or infected with acne due to food particles left clinging to the face.

Behavioral Problems

Pugs are not dogs that can be coaxed into doing tricks like playing fetch, no matter how nicely or sternly you ask. They are mildly stubborn that way and can be manipulative in order to get their way. Instilling discipline will be required of you to establish leadership. You will need to teach them, through uncompromised consistency that you mean business when you do.

Even if foods motivate your pugs, be mindful of how you hand out food rewards, because giving too much treats without the appropriate amount of physical activity or corresponding exercise can cause your Pug to gain unhealthy, unnecessary weight which may snowball to bigger health issues for your sweet-natured pal.

Housebreaking a Pug can be quite challenging because of its stubborn trait that's why you should employ maximum tolerance and great patience whenever you are housebreaking your Pug, your patience will later pay off if you do. You will have to expect four to six months of regular crate training before you see positive results.

A Pug emits all sorts of bodily sounds which some may find amusing and others may find gross or ill-mannered. Remember that the Pug cannot help making these noises due to their stubby faces and you will have to find the comical behind the wheezing, grunting, snoring, snorting and slobbering. This short list is not so much a list of issues of behavior. Rather, it is a list of physiological realities of the Pug dog which is part and parcel of this lovable canine.

Grooming Your Pug

The Pug is known for excessive shedding - stress on "excessive". For this reason, your Pug will need to be brushed daily to remove falling fur. Brushing your Pug can double as downtime quality time, which it will enjoy immensely if done in an atmosphere free of tension and stress.

Skin

Your Pug will require a nice, warm and bubbly bath at least every 3 weeks. It will be necessary to get the recommendation of your vet, a breeder or a seasoned guardian regarding the sort of shampoo to use for your buddy's baths. Do not make the mistake of using meant-for-human products as these can cause skin irritation to your canine.

Pugs have very sensitive skin and are prone to many skin conditions due to the folds of their skin. Germs and bacteria thrive and multiply quickly in the deep folds of its skin. Make certain that you clean its face, making sure to wipe between skin folds, as any food residue left could promote skin acne or pimples.

Eyes

You will want to pay mind to your Pugs eyes. The bulging feature of its eyes makes its peepers susceptible to debris entering its eyes which can lead to eye problems causing irritation and/or infections. Using a soft moistened cloth, gently wipe away the "gooey" build up around your Pugs eyes every day.

Ears

Regular ear cleaning once to two times a week is required to keep your Pug's ears free from wax and foreign elements that may have found its way there. This is also a good time to inspect your Pugs ears for irritation, excessive buildup of liquid wax or pus. These signs would indicate a necessary visit to the vet as these symptoms may be the onset of infections.

Nails

Pugs whose nails are left to grow long will be reason and cause for the canine to walk with an inconsistent gait which can lead to skeletal impairment.

Your Pug will need to get its nails trimmed every 3 to 6 months depending on how quickly its nails grow. A guardian should only attempt this grooming procedure with their new Pug after they have witnessed a professional do the job. Having a professional groomer accomplish this task will also allow you to find out which nail-cutting tool your Pug responds to with least resistance and opposition. Overcutting a nail is painful, causes bleeding and could lead to infection.

Chapter Seven: Showing Your Pug Dogs

The Pug is a wonderful dog to keep as a pet but this breed has the potential to be so much more than that. These dogs are very clever, active and trainable which makes them a great choice as a show dog. In order to show your Pug dogs, however, you have to make sure that he meets the requirements for the breed standard and you need to learn the basics about showing dogs.

In this chapter you will receive information about the breed standard for Pug breeds and you will find general information about preparing your dog for show.

Pug Dogs Breed Standard

The Pugs are an alert and enthusiastic breed that is accepted and recognized by the American Kennel Club (AKC). This section will give you the breed standard and general guidelines on how to present your dog.

Official Pug Dog Breed Standard

General Appearance:

The symmetry and overall appearance of the Pug are to be decidedly cubby and square. A Pug displayed as lean and leggy is highly objectionable as with a Pug who has short legs but has a long body.

Size, Proportion, Substance:

The Pug must be multum in parvo, and this condensation (if the word may be used) is apparent by compactness of form, well-knit measurements and hardness of developed muscle. A desirable weight of 14 - 18 pounds, whether dog or bitch, is the ideal weight. Its proportion is to be displayed square.

Head

The cranium of the Pug is massive, large and round. It is not to be apple-shaped and there is to be no indentation of the skull. The color of the eyes are dark, quite large, prominent and bold, it is to be globular in shape, solicitous and soft in expression, lustrous and full of fire when excited. The ears are small, soft, thin and has the feel of black velvet. Preference to the button ear is given. Wrinkles are deep and large. Its muzzle is blunt, square, short and not up faced. Its bite should be slightly undershot.

Neck, Topline, Body

The Pug's neck is to be slightly arched. It is to be strong and thick with enough length to carry the cranium proudly. The short back is even from the withers to the tail which is high set. The body of the Pug is to be cubby and short, wide in the chest are and well ribbed up. The tail of the Pug is curled as tightly as allowed over the canine's hip. A display of double curl is considered perfection.

Forequarters

The legs of the Pug are to be very strong, straight and of moderate length whilst set well under. Its elbows are to be directly beneath the withers when viewed from profile. Shoulders are to be moderately laid back. Pasterns are to be displayed strong, not steep or down. The feet of the Pug are neither very long like the foot of a hare, nor is it to be so round like those of a feline; toes are well split up, and nails are black and declaws are generally removed.

Hindquarters

The powerful and strong hindquarters of the Pug must have moderate bend of stifle and short hocks vertical to the ground. Legs are to display parallel when inspected from behind. Both hind and fore quarters are in harmony and balanced. Its thighs and buttocks are to be full and visibly muscular. Feet are as in front.

Coat

The Pug's coat is smooth, fine, short, soft and glossy. It is neither hard nor wooly.

Colour

The acceptable show colors are fawn or black. The fawn color is to be decided so to create complete contrast between the color, the trace and the mask.

Markings

The Pug's markings are to be clearly defined. The mask or muzzle, ears, moles on cheeks, thumb mark or diamond on forehead, the back should be as black as possible. The mask is to be black. The more intense and clearly defined it is, the better. The trace of the Pug is a black line which extends from the occiput to the tail.

Gait

When viewed from upfront, the Pugs forelegs are to be carried well forward, bearing no signs of weakness in the pasterns, with paws landing squarely and the central toes pointing straight ahead. The rear action must be strong and free through its hocks and stifles, sans twisting or turning in or out at the canine's joints. Its hind legs are to follow in line with the front legs. There is a mild natural convergence of the limbs both fore and aft. A modest roll of the hindquarters typifies the gait which is to be self-assured, jaunty and free.

Temperament

This breed is even-tempered, displaying stability, great charm, playfulness, dignity and possesses an outgoing and loving disposition.

Disqualification

Any other color other than black or fawn is disqualified.

Tips on Preparing Your Pug dogs for Show

Once you've determined that your Pug dogs achieved all the requirements of the breed standard, and then you can think about entering him in a dog show. Dog shows occur all year-round in many different locations so check the AKC or Kennel Club website for shows in your area. Remember, the rules for each show will be different so make sure to do your research so that you and your Pug are properly prepared for the show.

Here are some things you need to keep in mind while prepping your dog for show:

- Make sure that your Pug has been housetrained completely before registering him for a show.

- Ensure that your dog is properly socialized to be in an environment with many other dogs and people.

- Make sure that your Pug has had at least basic obedience training. He needs to respond to your commands and follow your lead in the show ring.

- Research the requirements for the individual show and make sure your Pug meets them before you register.

- Take your Pug to the vet to ensure that he is healthy enough for show and that he is caught up on his vaccinations – the bordatella vaccine is especially important since he'll be around a lot of other dogs.

- Pack a bag of supplies for things that you and your Pug are likely to need at the show.

- Have your Pug groomed the week of the show and take steps to make sure his coat stays in good condition.

Quick Checklist

Here are some things that may come in handy before, during and after the show:

- Registration information
- Dog crate or exercise pen
- Grooming table and grooming supplies
- Food and treats
- Food and water bowls
- Trash bags
- Medication (if needed)
- Change of clothes
- Food/water for self
- Paper towels or rags
- Toys for the dog

Chapter Eight: Breeding Your Pug Dogs

Breeding your Pug will entail a lot of foresight and preparation as well as a considerable chunk of money. Breeding will equate to vet bills you will have expect and foot. Newborn puppies need constant monitoring and gentle care which you may not be able to give if you are bound to a job that needs your regular presence and undistracted attention. The possibility of losing one or two or more puppies from a produced litter is a very real possibility that can take an emotional toll on the caregivers if they are not aware of what to expect. Should breeding your Pug be an avenue you want to explore later on, it will be imperative for you to do your homework and research further on to determine the right people to work with for an outcome that will bring about a higher likelihood of success.

This chapter aims to give basic canine mating and breeding information which can be a point of reference for the future. You will need to work closely with your vet if you do decide on breeding your Pug.

Basic Dog Breeding Information

There are vital health screening tests, including hip and elbow dysplasia that cannot be given until the canine turns two years old. Hence, most authorities of pets and aficionados recommend that male canines not be bred until it is at least a year and half in age, and female canines to not be mated or paired until they are on the second or third heat cycle, for health and behavioral reasons.

Before canines are bred an extensive evaluation and a thorough medical history of the mating canines should be determined. Of utmost importance is conducting screening tests for diseases which may have a genetic component. These screening tests may include pulmonary stenosis, ventricular septal defect, dilated cardiomyopathy, hemophilia, Von Willebrand's disease, epilepsy, hydrocephalus, intervertebral disk disease, mange, autoimmune skin disorders, hip dysplasia, elbow dysplasia, and a few more which you will want to go into detail with your vet.

Mating candidates should be scrutinized for congenital deformities such as cervical disc disease or an overshot jaw. An extensive family research must be conducted to determine or rule out genetic diseases which may potentially be inherited by the litter.

The female candidate's vagina should be scrutinized for any physical restrictions or structural hindrances which may impede a successful mating. The mammary glands are to be examined for any indications of abnormality. The testicles of the male candidate are to be examined and the health of their sperm as well as the canine's sperm count is to be evaluated.

If you are thinking of breeding purebred dogs, study up and familiarize yourself with the specific breeding standards accepted, recognized and approved by the various canine associations. Purebred dogs which are registered must comply with physical and temperament standards exacted by these clubs, and canines that do not satisfy these standards are not to be bred.

Mating Behaviour of Canines

Unlike women, female canines do not menstruate. What they experience instead is the heat cycle or the estrous cycle. When bitches are sexually mature they will experience this cycle twice a year. This cycle starts anywhere between the 9th and 12 month of your canine's life, however, this may vary from dog to dog. A dog's heat cycle has four stages: proestrus, estrus, diestrus and anestrus.

A variety of physical and hormonal events occur during each of these stages. Essential to a canine's heat cycle are three hormones; estrogen is responsible for the onset of the heat cycle; luteinizing hormone (LH) is elemental for ovulation; and progesterone is fundamental to maintaining the pregnancy.

The initial phase of a canine's heat, the proestrus, lasts about 9 days, however this length can range anywhere from 3 to 17 days. It is during this period when the canine's vulva becomes swollen and excretes a reddish-brown discharge. It is during this stage when the bitch is preparing itself for possible pregnancy. At this point the female canine will not yet be ready to accept a male.

The second phase of canine heat is estrus (not to be mistaken with "estrous" which is what the entire heat cycle is called) and lasts about 9 days but can happen within a period of 3 to 21 days. At this stage, the bitch will display a tender and swollen vulva and a vaginal discharge of variable reddish, pinkish or star color is apparent.

Estrogen levels will decrease in late proestrus. Luteinizing hormone (LH) sharply spike when estrogen falls and progesterone levels increase. For 2 to 3 days, at the surge of LH levels, females will become receptive to males. Many, but not collectively, female canines are playfully flirtatious during the estrus stage. She may prod the male with her nose, push her backside into the male's chest with her tail swept to one side.

Diestrusis the third phase of the heat cycle which ranges from 50-80 days, averaging a span of about 60 days. Whether the female has been bred or is pregnant the diestrus stage will commence. This stage of heat will have the bitch display signs of pregnancy. During these period females, pregnant or otherwise, may start "mothering" other animals, but will not reciprocate the advances of a male.

The fourth and last phrase of the heat cycle, the anestrus, can last from 130 to 250 days. During this stage of the heat cycle, females are not active sexually. This is phase where the body of the canine rests, and begins to prepare itself for the next cycle of heat.

Chapter Nine: Keeping Your Dog Healthy

The health of your Pug will greatly depend on a number of important factors you will need to research before making the decision to bring home one. Dealing with a reputable breeder is strongly suggested at this point as the future health of the puppy will hinge largely on the methods and procedures employed by the breeder.

A good breeder should be able to furnish health clearances for both the parents and the puppy you will be taking home. Health clearances will prove that a canine has been screened and cleared of a particular condition to which the canine is prone.

A future caregiver is to expect and get health clearances from the Pug breeders from the Auburn University for thrombopathia - a rare autosomal-recessive genetic form of hemophilia; from the Orthopedic Foundation for Animals (OFA) for von Willebrand's disease, elbow dysplasia, for hip dysplasia (with a score of fair or better), and hypothyroidism; and a certification from the Canine Eye Registry Foundation (CERF), stating that the eyes of the Pug are normal. You may confirm the authenticity of these clearances by checking the OFA website (offa.org).

Common Health Problems

Pug dogs are known to be a generally healthy breed, but like all canine breeds, they are prone to specific health conditions of which a potential caregiver wants to be aware. Not all Pugs will contract any or all the diseases it is prone to but it is vital for any future caregiver to know and understand these conditions to confidently recognize if their Pug suffers from such as well as to take the appropriate measures to avoid these instances.

Cheyletiella Dermatitis (Walking Dandruff)

This skin condition is caused by a tiny mite. Should you note a heavy presence of dandruff, especially down the midsection of the Pugs back, get in touch with your vet. The mites causing this condition are contagious, which will mean a household quarantine and treatment of all pets in the home.

Pug Dog Encephalitis

This disease (PDE) is a fatal brain disease causing the brain of the Pug dog to swell. There is very little known about the reason and causes why Pugs develop this condition, but seeming to have a genetic component, PDCA and the AKC sponsor research project aimed at learning the cause of this devastating disease. PDE often affects young pups, causing them to seize, circle, go blind, fall into coma and die within a few days or weeks of the onset.

Epilepsy

PDE is not the only disease to cause Pugs to seize; they are also prone to the condition known as idiopathic epilepsy or seizures for no apparent cause. If your Pug seizes, immediately take it to the vet to find solutions to appropriate treatments.

Nerve Degeneration

More mature Pugs which stagger, have trouble jumping up and down, drag their rears or become incontinent may suffer from nerve degeneration. The Pugs who are affected with this condition do not display pain or discomfort and the condition, if present in the Pug, slowly advances without notice. There is little known reason why this happens. To assist more mature Pug suffering from this condition, many guardians have bought and used carts to assist their Pugs mobility. Vets have may also give prescription medication to help alleviate the symptoms.

Corneal Ulcers

The Pugs eyes, because of its huge size and prominence, can easily be injured or develop ulcers on the clear part of the eye, or the cornea. Should your Pug squint or if its eyes appear red and excessively tear up, get in touch with your vet right away. Corneal ulcers respond well to medication, usually, when caught before it gets too severe. If this condition is left untreated, this can cause the Pug to go blind or even rupture the eye.

Dry Eye

Pigmentary keratitis and Keratoconjunctivitis sicca
are two dry-eye conditions noted in Pugs. They can happen
separately or at the same time. It is caused when the canine's
eyes don't produce enough tears to keep the eyes moist.
Your vet can perform screening test to determine if these
conditions are the cause of the dry-eye effect in your Pug,
and which can be controlled through medication. The
condition which causes black spots on the cornea and in the
corner of the eyes near to the nose is called pigmentary
keratitis and can cause blindness in the Pug if left untreated.
Your vet will be able to prescribe medication to keep the
Pugs eyes moistened and as well as dissolve the pigment to
avoid the spread of it. If a Pug suffers from these conditions,
these will require care and life-long therapy.

Eye Problems

Because of their large, protruding eyes, Pugs are
prone to a variety of eye problems, including distichiasis (an
abnormal growth of eyelashes on the margin of the eye,
resulting in the eyelashes rubbing against the eye);
distichiasis (an abnormal growth of eyelashes on the margin
of the eye, resulting in the eyelashes rubbing against the
eye); progressive retinal atrophy (a degenerative disease of

the retinal visual cells that leads to blindness); and entropion (the eyelid, usually the lower lid, rolls inward, causing the hair on the lid to rub on the eye and irritate it).

Allergies

There are a number of Pugs who suffer from a range of allergies from contact to food allergies. If you notice your Pug rubbing his face or licking its paws a great deal, suspect allergy as the culprit and have your canine go in for a checkup at the vet.

Demodectic Mange also known as Demodicosis

All dogs carry around with them a little passenger called a demodex mite. The dam or mother of the canine passes this on to the puppy litter and her offspring during the first few days of the puppy's lives. It is only the mother who passes this mite onto her litter; it is not contracted with exposure to other carrier dogs and it is not passed on to humans. These mites which live in hair follicles usually don't cause issues. However, if your Pug dog's immune system is weak or compromised; the canine can develop demodectic mange. This condition can be generalized or localized; the localized form displays in patches of red scaly skin accompanied by hair loss on the forelegs, neck and head. It is generally thought of as a puppy disease which most often clear ups by itself. Nevertheless, a Pug displaying these symptoms is still to be taken to the vet as this condition may aggravate to the generalized form of demodectic mange which covers the whole body and affects older puppies as well as young adult canines. In this case, the canine develops patchy skin, skin infections and bald spots all over its body. Due to the genetic link of this condition, the The American Academy of Veterinary Dermatology strongly recommends spaying or neutering all canines which develop generalized demodectic mange.

Staph Infection

This bacteria is usually found on skin, however, some dogs will break out in pimples and suffer infected hair follicles should it be found that their immune system suffer stress. Lesions appear to look like hives where hair is present; and on areas sans hair, the lesions have the appearance of ringworm. Contact your vet for the proper treatment of this condition.

Yeast Infection

Commonly affecting the armpits, feet, neck, inside the ears and the canine's groin, canine yeast infection manifests itself to the dog and through blackened, thickened skin. Your Pug will also smell bad if infected with this yeast condition. The best way to clear this up is to visit your vet. Prescribing medications will help clear up this condition.

Hemi-vertebrae

Snub-nosed or short-nosed breeds like French Bulldogs, Bulldogs and Pugs can possess misshapen vertebrae. There are occasions when only a few of the vertebrae are afflicted and the canine is able to live normally. However in other Pugs, between 4 to 6 months of life, this condition will cause them to display a weak gait and will seem uncoordinated as it staggers. A few of the dogs with this condition can get progressively ill and could even become paralyzed. The cause of the condition is unknown but it has been noted that surgery can help improve the quality of living of the Pug.

Hip Dysplasia

This canine malady affects small and large breeds alike and the Pug is prone to this. Factors such as environment, diet and importantly, genetics, are thought to contribute to this hip joint deformity. With proper vet attention and care, Pugs affected with this condition are often able to lead healthy, normal lives under the watchful care of a vet.

Legg-Perthes Diseases

Many toy breeds are prone to this other disease involving the hip joint. A Pug suffering from Legg-Perthes, decreases the blood supply to the head of the femur - or the large rear leg bone - and the head of the femur which is connected to the Pugs pelvis begins to disintegrate. Limping and atrophy of the leg muscle are the usual first signs of this condition and occur between the 4th and 6th month of the puppy's life. This condition can be corrected through surgery, cutting off the diseased femur so that it is no longer attached to the pelvis. Scar tissue resulting from the surgery creates a false joint and the puppy is usually pain free after healing.

Patellar Luxation

Patellar luxation is when the knee joint, often of the Pugs hind leg, slides in and out of place which causes pain in the canine. This can be a crippling condition; however, there are many dogs who lead normal lives with this condition.

Vaccination Sensitivity

Reports of sensitivity to routine vaccinations have been reported of Pugs. These symptoms usually include facial swelling, soreness, lethargy and hives. A canine sensitive to vaccines can develop complications from the vaccine and die, though this is quite rare. A potential caregiver should be watchful of a vaccinated Pug a few hours after the fact and should call the vet should anything unusual be noticed.

Recommended Vaccinations for Pug dogs

A newborn Pug usually has some immunity from the most common diseases to which canines are prone to from its mother. Ideally the dam of the Pug should have been receiving inoculation throughout her life and she will in turn pass onimmunity to her litter of puppies within the first 48 hours of the pup's life via the colostrum found in her milk.

Pups will receive from their mother, varying amounts of antibodies, but this initial immunity will start to wear off between the 5th and 6th week of the puppies lives. The wear off period varies from puppy to puppy within the same liter. One pup may enjoy immunity from parvo for 8 weeks whilst others from the same litter could be prone to parvo by the 5th week. Length of immunity is all dependent on the antibodies each pup receives while it nurses with its mother.

This uneven and immeasurable distribution of immunity is reason to start vaccinating puppies whilst the puppies are young and maintenance is to be continued by giving those vaccinations several times throughout their lives. Doing so will guarantee that each of the puppies are getting the immunity it needs through vaccination, which otherwise naturally wears off, until the canine is able to begin to produce its own antibodies.

There are two practiced protocols suggested for puppies and these would depend on the protocol your vet follows. The age of the Pug is the foremost difference between the two protocols. The first protocol proposes that the puppies start getting their shots when they reach the 5th week of their lives. The other protocol advocates that the pups start getting their shots between the 8th and 9th week of life.

Your breeder may give recommendation to start shots at week 5 of your Pugs life and may have most likely begun administering the initial vaccination before you take home your puppy. On the other hand, your vet may recommend giving the shots later. As future guardian, you will have to decide early on which protocol you think is best. Better yet, have the breeder and your vet talk to each other and work something out before the administration of vaccine is on the table.

Almost all vets, breeders, and seasoned pet caregivers agree on the initial vaccination structure consisting of the vital "core" shots which are meant to protect your puppy; hepatitis, canine distemper, parvovirus and rabies are all considered to be the important core vaccinations your Pug should absolutely have to be protected from these diseases.

Vaccinations considered as "non-core" shots include canine adenovirus-2, leptospirosis, bordetella, coronavirus, parainfluenza, lyme disease and measles. These vaccines, while still important, are not as essential as the primary core shots. Many if not most vets will still suggest that your Pug be vaccinated against these, and in addition, pet care facilities and pet boarding "hotels" would actually require show of proof that the canine had received these shots for you and your canine to enjoy the services they offer.

A typical vaccination timetable for a Pug puppy who starts its vaccinations at the 5th week of life will appear this way:

5 weeks: Parvovirus vaccination

6 and 9 weeks: Combination vaccines would usually include hepatitis, parainfluenza, parvovirus, canine distemper and adenovirus. The coronavirus could be incorporated during this time should it be a concern, however, the coronavirus is a disease most notably seen in newborn puppies.

12 weeks: Rabies vaccine is to be administered by the vet

12-16 weeks: A combination of vaccines against leptospirosis, lyme disease and if necessary, the coronavirus vaccine is administered.

Once your Pug reaches its year-old milestone, it will need booster shots which can be given in combination shots. Talk to your vet and talk about giving your dog these booster shots in alternating years because it has been evidenced that immunity lasts longer than a year for these vaccines. This spread out of vaccine administration puts less stress on the Pugs immune system.

Rabies is a required and necessary shot to be given every 2-3 years. Frequency of rabies vaccination will depend on the laws of the state in which you reside. To determine this, research on the frequency your state requires.

Bordetella vaccination, or nasal injection will need to be administered more dogs who will participate in dog shows and/or if the dog is foreseen to spend periods of time in a boarding kennel. Canines can easily catch and spread respiratory diseases or spread kennel cough if they spend periods of time sharing closed quarters in the company of other canines. Commonly, these are not fatal but can make your Pug dog pretty sick. Boarding kennels and pet hotels require that dogs are vaccinated against bordetella before they are allowed lodging in their facilities.

Keep in mind that the Pug will not be immediately protected against a particular disease the minute it gets the vaccination. It will usually take several to up to 14 days before your Pug canine is able to produce the antibodies it will require to have immunity against a disease.

That being said, if you get your Pug vaccinated, say, against distemper or another disease, you shouldn't be too quick to rush out and risk exposing it to other dogs. Hold off too on taking your newly vaccinated Pug to locations where a higher chance of exposure to diseases is imminent. Employ caution and common sense when protecting your Pug's health and wellness.

Signs of Possible Illness

Knowing a little more about medical conditions your Pug may be prone to is a chunk of information to store away for future reference. As with us humans, a canine's health will change over time. Sadly, our four-legged, furry pals age much faster than we. You are still reading this because you have your heart set on keeping a Pug for company. No matter the age of your canine, keep in mind that you play a very large role in keeping her healthy and fight off illnesses. She may not be able to tell you in a language you'd understand but she will certainly display signs unusual that would give cause to pay heed.

Should you notice any or most of these, bring your pug to the vet immediately:

- excessive drinking or urination
- a change in energy or activity level; a lack of interest doing things they used to enjoy
- sleeping more than usual; a shift in attitude; behavioral change
- dry, itchy skin, lumps, sores and head shaking
- eyes which are cloudy or red
- bad breath or drooling

- change in appetite; weight gain or loss
- difficulty getting up from a lying position and vice versa; stiffness in movements
- labored breathing, excessive panting, coughing, sneezing.
- Frequent stomach problems; digestive upsets and/changes in bowel movements.

Chapter Ten: Pug Dogs Care Sheet

You are almost done with this little book of Pug information. Having come this far may mean that you, dear reader, are a step closer to making the Pug your definite choice for a new home companion and pet buddy. It is the fervent prayer of this author that you have been enlightened by the Pug-full information which aims to get you ready as you eagerly anticipate taking on the tasks of being caregiver to your awaited Pug.

Do keep in mind some of the more important things that you will need to adhere to successfully raise your Pug healthy, happy and well-rounded. Deal only with reputable breeders who will include you with each tiny milestone as you wait expectantly on your Pug. Make sure that all transactions, agreements and monies exchanged are documented, dated and recorded. Deal with breeders who screen new pups for possible inherited, genetic or acquired diseases. Make sure that results of tests are furnished to you, certificates of clean health are provided to you (in fact, this is something you want to clarify upfront before making any binding commitments).

Work with a trusted, well-experienced vet who will proactively provide only the best health care fit for your precious pet.

Pug Information Sheet

- Scientific Name: Canis lupus familiaris
- Breed Size: small-sized
- Height: 10 inches to 1 foot, 2 inches tall at the shoulder
- Weight: 14 - 18 pounds
- Physique: small
- Coat Length: short and smooth

- Skin Texture: soft and silky
- Color: black, fawn, apricot fawn, white,
- Tail: short and curls into its hips
- Temperament: friendly, loyal, jovial, and is happiest when around their caregivers.
- Strangers: will excessively bark at people at the door, most specially strangers
- Children: older children from 11 up.
- Other Pets: gets along well with other with proper socialization and ample time
- Exercise Needs: walking and playing
- Health Conditions: prone to certain canine diseases and health problems
- Lifespan: average 9 to 15 years

Nutritional Needs

- Nutritional Needs: protein, carbohydrates, fats, vitamins and minerals, water
- Amount to Feed (puppy): 10 grams
- Amount to Feed (adult): 12.5 grams
- Important Minerals:
  Vitamin A (Retinol, beta carotene as precursor)
  Vitamin D (Calciferol)
  Vitamin E (Tocopherol)
  Vitamin K (Naphthoquinone)

Vitamin B1 (Thiamine)

Vitamin B2 (Riboflavin)

Vitamin B3 (Niacin)

Vitamin B5 (Pantothenic Acid)

- Measure of serving per meal:

½ cup of food for 1 pound puppy

1 cup of food for 3 pounds puppy

25 cups of food for 5 pound puppy

2 cups of food for 6 pounds puppy

- Types of Dog Food:

Dry: 75 to 80 % water, 8 - 15% protein and 2 - 15% fat

Semi-moist Food: 15-25% protein, 5-10% fat, 25-35% carbohydrates, and 30% water

Canned Food: 75% moisture

Food Additives: Antioxidants, Herbs, Flavors and Extracts

Feeding bulk/day: the recommended daily bulk of food to a Pug adult is ¼ to ½ cup of high quality dry food in two meals

Breeding Information

- Menstruation period: two to three weeks
- Sexual Maturity (female): 5-12 months
- Sexual Maturity (male): 5 months
- Breeding Age (female): 14 months
- Breeding Age (male): 16 months
- Litter Size: about 4-6 puppies
- Birth Interval: 15 – 30 minutes
- Pregnancy: 63 days
- Puppy Birth Weight: 75g to 350g

Dog Accessories

- Food and Water Bowls: Stainless or Ceramic
- Toys: teething toys, chewable toys, speaking and moving toys, kong, etc.
- Dog Bed: of average size
- Other accessories: Y-shaped harness, grooming tools and cleaning supplies, etc.

Index

C

D

H

I

K

L

Q

R

S

T

U

V

W

Photo Credits

Page 1 Photo by Unsplash via Pixabay.com,

https://pixabay.com/en/pug-puppy-dog-animal-cute-690566/

Page 10 Photo by Pravin 73 via Pixabay.com,

https://pixabay.com/en/pug-cute-dog-2112174/

Page 24 Photo by Unsplash via Pixabay.com,

https://pixabay.com/en/pug-dog-pet-animal-puppy-cute-801826

Page 39 Photo by ifd_Photography via Pixabay.com,

https://pixabay.com/en/puggle-dog-smiling-moby-funny-2228841/

Page 46 Photo by woodsilver via Pixabay.com,

https://pixabay.com/en/dog-pug-training-jumping-breed-2105686/

Page 61 Photo by SNGPhotography via Pixabay.com,

https://pixabay.com/en/puppy-bone-dog-pet-animal-food-1502565/

Page 71 Photo by winterseitler via Pixabay.com,

https://pixabay.com/en/old-man-pug-park-dog-character-2090377/

Page 79 Photo by Katrinbechtel via Pixabay.com,

https://pixabay.com/en/pug-meadow-dog-2035675/

Page 87 Photo by kennedyfotos via Pixabay.com,

https://pixabay.com/en/pug-dog-cute-adorable-canine-2223195/

Page 93 Photo by Incygneia via Pixabay.com,

https://pixabay.com/en/pug-dog-happy-smiling-pet-965766/

Page 110 Photo by tpsdave via Pixabay.com,

https://pixabay.com/en/dogs-pugs-cute-together-nature-82799/

References

Pug Temperament, What's Good About 'Em, What's Bad About 'Em – YourPureBredPuppy.com

http://www.yourpurebredpuppy.com/reviews/pugs.html

Pug - Temperament & Personality – Petwave.com

http://www.petwave.com/Dogs/Breeds/Pug/Personality.aspx

Pug – DogBreedInfo.com

http://www.dogbreedinfo.com/pug.htm

Why Pugs Dogs Are the Perfect Family Pet – PetHelpful.com

https://pethelpful.com/dogs/Why-Pugs-Dogs-Are-The-Perfect-Family-Pet

Pug Dog Breed Information and Personality Traits – Hillspet.com

http://www.hillspet.com/en/us/dog-breeds/pug

Don't Get Pug – PugVillage.com

http://www.pugvillage.com/general/dont-get-pug

Pug Temperament, Understand Your Dog – PugTips.com

http://pugtips.com/breed-temperament/

Pug Dog Behavior – PetPugDog.com

http://www.petpugdog.com/pug-dog-behavior-
temperament

Pug – Wikipedia.org

https://en.wikipedia.org/wiki/Pug

Pug History: Breed Origin – PugTips.com

http://pugtips.com/history/

History of the Pug – Petcha.com

https://www.petcha.com/history-of-the-pug/

Meet the Pug – AKC.org

http://www.akc.org/dog-breeds/pug/detail/

History – Pugminded.com

http://pugminded.com/ahistoryofpugs.html

The History of the Pug – PugVillage.com

http://www.pugvillage.com/your-first-pug/history-pug

The Pug Dog Heat Cycle – PetPugDog.come

http://www.petpugdog.com/pug-heat-cycle

Breeding Pugs — Introduction to Pug Breeding – BreedingBusiness.com

https://breedingbusiness.com/breeding-pugs-introduction/

Mating and Pregnancy Stages Explained and items you will need – SweetPeaPugs.co.uk

http://www.sweetpeapugs.co.uk/mating--pregnancy-stages.html

Feeding – PugDogClub.org.uk

http://pugdogclub.org.uk/about-pugs/caring-for-your-pug/feeding/

Nutrition for Dogs and What It Means For Your Pug – I-Love-Pugs.com

http://www.i-love-pugs.com/nutrition-for-dogs.html

Pug Breed Standard – AKC.org

http://images.akc.org/pdf/breeds/standards/Pug.pdf

Get Help with Pug Health Problems to Keep Your Dog In Good Shape – PugProblems.com

http://www.pugproblems.com/health-issues/

Pug Dog Health Problems – Pets4Homes.co.uk

https://www.pets4homes.co.uk/pet-advice/pug-dog-health-problems.html

Feeding Baby
Cynthia Cherry
978-1941070000

Axolotl
Lolly Brown
978-0989658430

Dysautonomia, POTS
Syndrome
Frederick Earlstein
978-0989658485

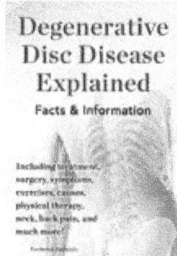

Degenerative Disc
Disease Explained
Frederick Earlstein
978-0989658485

Sinusitis, Hay Fever,
Allergic Rhinitis Explained
Frederick Earlstein
978-1941070024

Wicca
Riley Star
978-1941070130

Zombie Apocalypse
Rex Cutty
978-1941070154

Capybara
Lolly Brown
978-1941070062

Eels As Pets
Lolly Brown
978-1941070167

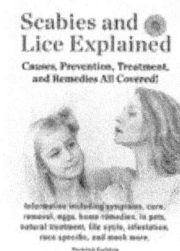

Scabies and Lice Explained
Frederick Earlstein
978-1941070017

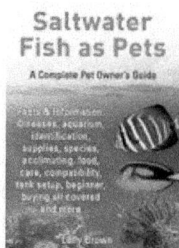

Saltwater Fish As Pets
Lolly Brown
978-0989658461

Torticollis Explained
Frederick Earlstein
978-1941070055

Kennel Cough
Lolly Brown
978-0989658409

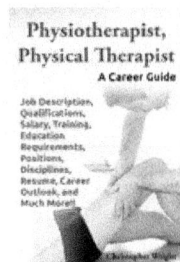

Physiotherapist, Physical
Therapist
Christopher Wright
978-0989658492

Rats, Mice, and Dormice
As Pets
Lolly Brown
978-1941070079

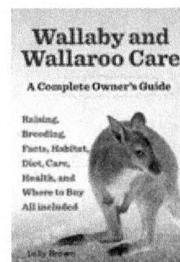

Wallaby and Wallaroo Care
Lolly Brown
978-1941070031

Bodybuilding Supplements
Explained
Jon Shelton
978-1941070239

Demonology
Riley Star
978-19401070314

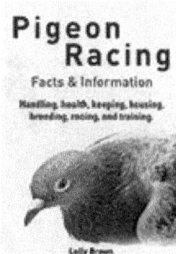

Pigeon Racing
Lolly Brown
978-1941070307

Dwarf Hamster
Lolly Brown
978-1941070390

Cryptozoology
Rex Cutty
978-1941070406

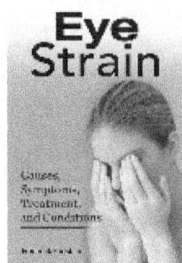

Eye Strain
Frederick Earlstein
978-1941070369

Inez The Miniature Elephant
Asher Ray
978-1941070353

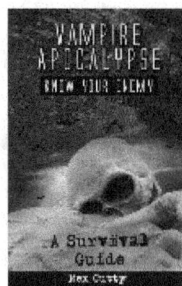

Vampire Apocalypse
Rex Cutty
978-1941070321

www.ingramcontent.com/pod-product-compliance
Lightning Source LLC
LaVergne TN
LVHW051643080426
835511LV00016B/2462